THE *South Carolina* COLONY

Our Thirteen Colonies

SPIRIT
of America®

THE *South Carolina* COLONY

By Jean F. Blashfield

Content Adviser: Eric Gilg, Department of History, University of
Massachusetts, Amherst, Massachusetts

The Child's World®
Chanhassen, Minnesota

8

THE *South Carolina* COLONY

Published in the United States of America by The Child's World®
PO Box 326 • Chanhassen, MN 55317-0326 • 800-599-READ • www.childsworld.com

Acknowledgments

The Child's World®: Mary Berendes, Publishing Director

Editorial Directions, Inc.: E. Russell Primm, Editorial Director; Melissa McDaniel, Line Editor; Elizabeth K. Martin, Assistant Editor; Olivia Nellums, Editorial Assistant; Susan Hindman, Copy Editor; Joanne Mattern, Proofreader; Kevin Cunningham, Peter Garnham, Ruthanne Swiatkowski, Fact Checkers; Tim Griffin/IndexServ, Indexer; Cian Loughlin O'Day, Photo Researcher; Linda S. Koutris, Photo Selector

Photo

Cover: North Wind Picture Archives; Bettmann/Corbis: 6, 12, 13, 24, 34; Corbis: 7 (Mark A. Johnson), 9 (Dewitt Jones), 11 (Kevin Fleming), 14, 22, 23, 26, 27 (Raymond Gehman), 29, 35 (The Stapleton Collection); Getty Images/Hulton Archive: 15, 17, 19, 21, 25, 30, 32; North Wind Picture Archives: 8, 18, 20; Stock Montage: 16, 28, 31.

Library of Congress Cataloging-in-Publication Data
Blashfield, Jean F.
  The South Carolina Colony / by Jean F. Blashfield.
    p. cm. — (Our colonies)
  "Spirit of America."
  Includes bibliographical references (p.) and index.
  Contents: South Carolina's Indians—The challenge of settlement—Struggle, growth, and prosperity—South Carolina at war—A new state, a new nation—Time line—Glossary terms.
  ISBN 1-56766-710-4 (alk. paper)
  1. South Carolina—History—Colonial period, ca. 1600–1775—Juvenile literature. 2. South Carolina—History—1775–1865—Juvenile literature. [1. South Carolina—History—Colonial period, ca. 1600–1775. 2. South Carolina—History—1775–1865.] I. Title. II. Series.
  F272.B57 2003
  975.7'02—dc21   2003003776

12 22 26

Contents

Chapter ONE

Native American Life

PEOPLE HAVE LIVED IN THE AREA NOW CALLED South Carolina since 8000 B.C. Over time, the native people of South Carolina began living in villages. Some villages housed only one large family. Others were home to several thousand people.

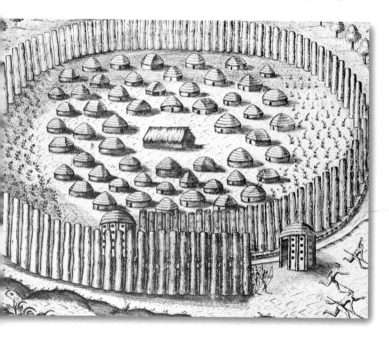

Native Americans in South Carolina's Low Country surrounded their villages with high fences called palisades.

In the coastal region, called the Low Country, native people surrounded their villages with high log fences called palisades. They built huts that had roofs of palm leaves spread across branches. Palm leaves woven into mats were used as walls. These mats could be

taken down. The people of the mountainous regions, called the Up Country, built similar houses. They also made walls of woven mats, but their walls could not be taken down. Instead, the walls were coated with mud to keep out the cold.

Native American men hunted deer, bear, wild turkeys, and bison in the area that would become South Carolina. At the time, bison roamed throughout the Southeast. When white hunters began to kill them in large numbers, these great beasts moved west.

Interesting Fact

▶ The Catawba people refer to themselves as *yeh is-WAH h'reh,* which translates to mean the "people of the river." Before the Europeans arrived, the Catawbas numbered in the hundreds of thousands. But by 1826, that number had dwindled to only about 110. Today, their population is growing again.

▶ The "thunder of the plains" was a name often used to describe the huge herds of bison that roamed across the North American wilderness.

The early native people of South Carolina also fished, usually with spears. They moved among the islands and on the rivers in canoes carved from thick pine or cypress logs.

The women grew corn, beans, and squash. They also grew a little tobacco, which they smoked for religious reasons. Some native women kept herds of deer, which they milked. They also tanned deer hides into buckskin for clothing. Cherokee

Bison were plentiful in the area that would become South Carolina until white hunters began killing large numbers of them.

trousers, shirts, and moccasins later became the common clothing for Europeans living in the American wilderness. Native women wore buckskin skirts and capes in winter, but in summer they wore little but moccasins.

In the 1500s, the largest native group in this area were the Cherokee. The Cherokee lived in the Up Country. They often fought with the neighboring Catawba people, South Carolina's second-largest native group.

Native Americans used deerskins to make clothing.

About 29 separate groups of Native Americans lived in South Carolina when Europeans first arrived there. Most of the smaller groups disappeared. Some may have merged with the larger groups. But many Native Americans were killed by diseases they caught from the Europeans. They had never been exposed to these diseases before, so their bodies could not fight them. Across the continent, millions of Native Americans died from European diseases.

South Carolina Colony at time of the first European settlement

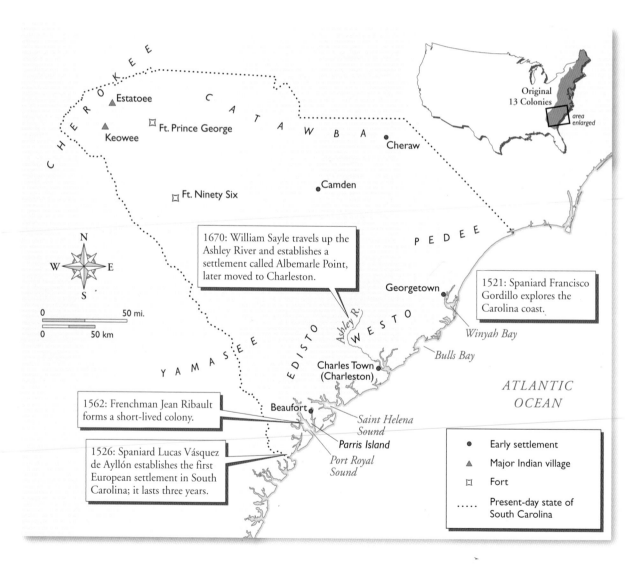

Original 13 Colonies

area enlarged

Estatoee

Keowee

Ft. Prince George

Ft. Ninety Six

Camden

Cheraw

1670: William Sayle travels up the Ashley River and establishes a settlement called Albemarle Point, later moved to Charleston.

Georgetown

1521: Spaniard Francisco Gordillo explores the Carolina coast.

Winyah Bay

Bulls Bay

Charles Town (Charleston)

ATLANTIC OCEAN

1562: Frenchman Jean Ribault forms a short-lived colony.

Beaufort

Saint Helena Sound

1526: Spaniard Lucas Vásquez de Ayllón establishes the first European settlement in South Carolina; it lasts three years.

Parris Island

Port Royal Sound

- Early settlement
▲ Major Indian village
◻ Fort
..... Present-day state of South Carolina

THE NATIVE AMERICANS OF THE SOUTHEAST HAVE A RICH AND VARIED culture. At the time Europeans first arrived in North America, the native people played the game now known as lacrosse. Each player carried a wooden stick with a net or small basket attached to one end. They used these racquets to carry or throw a small ball—no hands allowed! Many people of the Southeast played a version of this game with two simple sticks, one in each hand. They moved the ball by balancing it between the two sticks.

Dancing is a central part of Cherokee culture. One dance important to the Cherokee is the Stomp Dance. The Stomp Dance is like a rhythmic Follow the Leader. The leader makes up his own rhythmic pattern. The dancers choose their own movements in time to the leader's songs. Both men and women dance, but it is women who usually serve as the rhythm section. They dance wearing rattles made of turtle shells around their ankles and wrists.

Chapter TWO

The Europeans Arrive

Christopher Columbus lands on the Caribbean island he named San Salvador in 1492.

THE SPANIARDS WERE THE FIRST EUROPEANS to explore the area now known as South Carolina. After explorer Christopher Columbus arrived in the Caribbean Sea in 1492, the Spanish laid claim to the islands

in this area. Over the years, the Spanish sent more explorers to other parts of North America.

King Charles I of Spain (above) granted the eastern coast of North America to Lucas Vásquez de Ayllón.

The first European to explore the Carolina coast was Francisco Gordillo in 1521. He had been sent by Lucas Vásquez de Ayllón, a wealthy land-owner on the island of Hispaniola, which is now Haiti and the Dominican Republic. Based on Gordillo's voyage, Spain claimed the eastern coast of North America.

Along the Carolina coast, Gordillo invited some Native Americans aboard his ship for a feast. But once they were on board, he sailed away, kidnapping them to use as slaves. Ayllón was furious at Gordillo. He ordered that the Native Americans be returned to their home-land. Gordillo did as he was told, but one native man chose to stay. He became a Christ-ian and was given the new name Francisco Chicora. Chicora accompanied Ayllón to Spain, where he was put on public display.

The king of Spain granted the land that Gordillo had explored to Ayllón. Ayllón then found 500 citizens of Hispaniola willing to be

Interesting Fact

▶ Francisco Chicora was known to weave incredible stories about the region he came from. He told Allyón that his people were ruled by a giant king and that life was easy for everyone. This in-spired Allyón to travel to the Americas himself.

13

The swampy land in Carolina made life difficult for the early settlers.

settlers. In the summer of 1526, they established the village of San Miguel de Guadalupe. Historians disagree over where the village was located. Many say that it was in South Carolina, but others say it was in Georgia.

The swamps, summer heat, and terrible insects made building difficult. Within weeks, the settlers began to die. Ayllón himself was the first to die of **malaria.** Many other settlers in the small village also died. The remaining colonists decided too many had died, and so they abandoned Carolina and returned to Hispaniola.

No one else settled in Carolina until 1562. That year, a French naval officer, Jean Ribault, sailed into Port Royal Sound with 150 people. These settlers were mostly Huguenots, French Protestants who were mistreated in Catholic France. Native Americans helped the new settlers build a fort on Parris Island.

Ribault went back to France, thinking that he would return with more settlers and supplies. But the settlers had many problems after he left. They did not have enough food, and some of the men died. The remaining men rebelled against the captain left in charge and decided to try to sail home. They were on the verge of dying at sea when an English ship rescued them.

The Spanish were furious when they learned about the French settlement, because they thought the land was theirs. They built forts along the eastern coast from Florida to Carolina. Two forts, San Filipe and San Marcos, were built on Parris Island. Native Americans burned San Filipe. Then, in 1587, the Spanish king, busy fighting wars at home, ordered his soldiers to withdraw from San Marcos. It was almost 100 years before Europeans again tried to settle in Carolina.

Jean Ribault led a group of French Huguenots who landed in South Carolina in 1562.

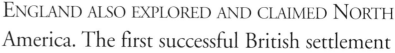

Chapter THREE

Struggle and Growth

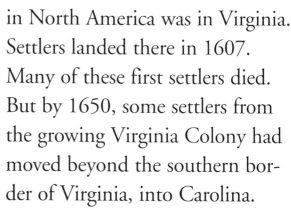

ENGLAND ALSO EXPLORED AND CLAIMED NORTH America. The first successful British settlement in North America was in Virginia. Settlers landed there in 1607. Many of these first settlers died. But by 1650, some settlers from the growing Virginia Colony had moved beyond the southern border of Virginia, into Carolina.

In 1663, King Charles II of England gave Carolina to eight men. These eight men were called the Lords **Proprietors.** They controlled all the land in Carolina and could sell it to whomever they chose. They decided to let people of any religion buy land

16

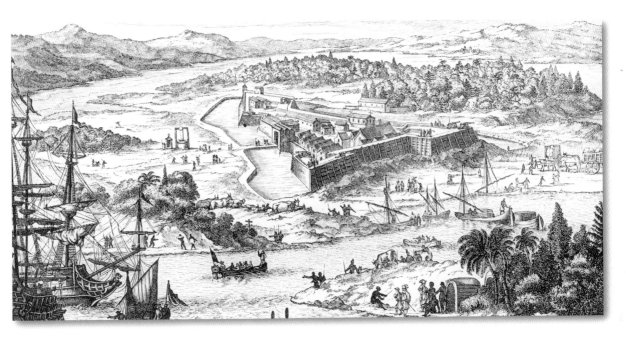

The settlement of Charleston, South Carolina, in 1673

in their colony. This freedom of religion, which was unusual in the American colonies, attracted many people to Carolina.

In 1670, William Sayle led a group of settlers up the Ashley River. They established a village called Albemarle Point. They later moved their settlement to where the Cooper and Ashley Rivers join. Their new town was called Charles Town—later Charlestown, then Charleston.

The next year, Sir John Yeamans arrived in the small village with a shipload of enslaved black people from Africa. Each colonist who bought a slave was given more land. From the beginning, then, slavery was an

Interesting Fact

▸ Trade in deerskins was big business on many South Carolina rivers. The many hides shipped to England often ended up being dyed purple or yellow and then made into breeches, or knee-length pants, for fashionable Englishmen known as "dandies."

Settlers in South Carolina refused to let the Lords Proprietors take control of the colony.

important part of the colony's economy and culture.

Settlers in Carolina established an **assembly,** which met in Charleston. But the Lords Proprietors had planned for Carolina to be governed directly from England. In 1687, the Proprietors tried to take control. The settlers, however, firmly pointed out that Carolina's original **charter** called for laws to be confirmed by all white male landowners. The eight Proprietors had to give in. They could choose only the governor of the colony.

In 1703, Sir Nathaniel Johnson became governor of Carolina. He did not believe that the colonists should have the right to worship as they pleased. He convinced the assembly to pass a law requiring men who served in the assembly to be members of the Church of England. The colonists had to go to **Parliament** to regain freedom of religion.

By 1700, about half the people in South Carolina were enslaved workers. Many of the slaves were Native Americans, rather than Africans. South Carolina was the center of the Native American slave trade. Most were sent to the Caribbean, where they worked on sugar plantations, which are large farms, and in mines. Many, though, were kept in South Carolina to work on rice plantations.

Some historians believe that Africans introduced rice farming to South Carolina. The area's swampy ground was excellent for growing rice. One type of rice was native to

Interesting Fact

▶ In the last half of the 1600s, many Native Americans were sold into slavery by their own people. They were handed over to the Europeans in exchange for things like guns, cloth, and beads. This practice abruptly ended in 1715.

The Indigo Expert

ELIZA LUCAS WAS THE DAUGHTER OF A WEALTHY British army officer who owned several plantations near Charleston. She was only 16 when he became the governor of the Caribbean island of Antigua in 1738. He left Eliza in charge of his Carolina plantations.

Eliza's father sent her some seeds of the indigo plant. It produces pea-like pods from which a blue dye is made. Eliza experimented with growing plants. She bred indigo plants that would grow in the light soil of the Up Country. She gave her neighbors some of the plants. Soon, all over the Up Country, enslaved workers were tending indigo plants. By the time Eliza married at age 22, South Carolina had become an important source of the dye for people around the world. Indigo was now a big part of the South Carolina economy.

19

the area. But the rice that Carolinians grew may have developed from a bag of seed that a sea captain brought from the island of Madagascar, off the coast of Africa.

Many enslaved people on the rice plantations died from overwork, but the plantation owners quickly replaced them with new workers they had bought or kidnapped. Sometimes, the slaves rose up against the plantation owners. In 1739, 100 slaves killed 30 whites in what was called the Stono Rebellion.

Carolina was attracting settlers. Many Scots came from Scotland. More Huguenots came from France. Jews were kept out of most

Enslaved workers sometimes died of overwork on plantations in Carolina

American colonies, but they were welcome in Carolina. Another religious group, the Quakers, also came to Carolina from northern colonies where they were not welcome.

Most new settlers moved to the southern part of Carolina, especially around Charleston. Over time, "South" Carolina became much wealthier than "North" Carolina. The Lords Proprietors divided the colony in half in 1712. Though it was still officially a single British colony, it had two governors.

Even though more people were coming to the colony, it was still a dangerous place. For 10 months starting in 1715, the Yamasee people and the white colonists fought. The Yamasee believed they had been treated badly

George Fox (standing on chair) was the founder of the Society of Friends, or Quakers. The Quakers came to Carolina from colonies in the north where they were not welcome.

by the traders who bought furs from them. By the end of the war, about 400 colonists had been killed. The Yamasee who survived were driven south into Florida. This war left the young colony seriously in debt. The colonists were also hungry because no crops had been planted during the fighting. The Lords Proprietors refused to help the colony—they saw their role as one of getting money (from land sales), not giving money. When Charleston came under frequent attack by pirates, the Proprietors again failed to help.

In 1719, the colonists asked King George I (above) to make the southern part of Carolina a royal colony.

In 1719, the colonists appealed to King George I to make the southern part of Carolina a royal colony. This would mean that South Carolina would be ruled by the king, not the Lords Proprietors. In 1729, North and South Carolina officially became two separate colonies.

During the following decades, Great Britain struggled against France for control of parts of North America. In 1754, this struggle turned into the French and Indian War. The issue was finally settled when Britain won the war in 1763, gaining control of Canada and all land east of the Mississippi River.

Most American colonists were pleased with the result of the war. But they weren't so pleased when the British wanted them to pay the cost of the war. That idea would eventually lead to more war—and a new nation.

Life in the Up Country

THE RICE PLANTATIONS OF THE LOW COUNTRY DEPENDED ON ENSLAVED WORKERS. But away from the coast, in the Up Country, farmers needed fewer slaves to grow their indigo. They depended on their families to do much of the farmwork. They grew crops for their own use or to trade with neighbors.

Families in the Up Country tended to be quite large. Farmers wanted to have many children to help out on the farm and around the house. Few of these children were able to attend school. Those who learned to read had been taught by their parents. Slaves in the Up Country, like slaves elsewhere in the colonies, were not allowed to be educated.

Chapter FOUR

South Carolina at War

MANY COLONISTS, ESPECIALLY IN THE NORTH, became angry when the British taxed the colonies to pay for the French and Indian War. The colonists thought this was unfair because no one represented them in Parliament, so they had no say in what laws were passed.

The first of these taxes was the Stamp Act, which Parliament passed in 1765. It required people to buy a stamp to be put on all official papers and newspapers. A supply of the stamps arrived by ship in Charleston. A group of men calling themselves the Sons of Lib-

A cartoon showing opposition to the Stamp Act

This is the Place to affix the STAMP.

An Exact Prospect of CHARLES TOWN, the Metropolis of the Province of SOUTH CAROLINA.

erty hanged a dummy dressed like a government official. Frightened, the government officials hid the stamps.

The British were persuaded to end the stamp tax. But they soon called for other taxes. They taxed cloth, tea, glass, lead, and even paint. The tea tax brought on the famous Boston Tea Party in Massachusetts. On December 16, 1773, some Bostonians dressed as Native Americans went aboard a ship. They dumped cases of tea into Boston Harbor. South Carolina had a similar, but less famous, event—the Charleston Tea Party in 1774.

The British sent troops to take control of Boston. Angry colonists organized a meeting of all colonies in Philadelphia, Pennsylvania.

When a supply of stamps arrived in Charleston, South Carolina (above), by ship, the Sons of Liberty protested.

25

Colonists in Boston, Massachusetts, dumped cases of tea into the harbor in protest of British taxes. This event became known as the Boston Tea Party.

This First **Continental Congress** wrote a protest letter. In it, they pointed out that they deserved the same rights as Englishmen who lived in Britain. The king and Parliament ignored the protest.

The first gunfire of the war—the "shot heard 'round the world"—was in Massachusetts in April 1775. The next month, the Continental Congress met again in Philadelphia. On June 15, 1775, they created an army, with George Washington at its head. South Carolina created its own militia, a local army, ready to fight with Washington. The war was on.

In the Up Country, war broke out between Loyalists (people who supported the British) and Patriots (people who supported independence). In November 1775, hundreds of Loyalists and Patriots fought in western South Carolina, near the town of Ninety Six. It was the first land battle of the Revolution fought in the South.

As the war was beginning, South Carolinians formed their own independent state by writing a **constitution.** It went into effect on

Visitors can visit the Revolutionary War battlefield at the Ninety Six National Historic Site in South Carolina.

▶ During the Revolutionary War, South Carolina had a few Patriot rebels who were as sly as foxes. They excelled at tracking and sneaking up on the British in swamps, mountains, and marshes. Most acquired colorful nicknames too, such as Thomas "The Gamecock" Sumter, Andrew "Fighting Elder" Pickens, and Francis "the Swamp Fox" Marion.

March 21, 1776. John Rutledge was elected president of the new General Assembly.

Almost four months later, the Continental Congress approved the Declaration of Independence. That vote in Philadelphia had not been easy. In a rough first vote, South Carolina's Edward Rutledge (John's younger brother) voted against independence. But on July 2, when the final vote was taken, he

John Rutledge was elected president of the General Assembly of the independent state of South Carolina in 1776.

voted in favor. He didn't want South Carolina to be the only state voting against independence. At 27, he was the youngest person to sign the Declaration of Independence.

Though the colonies had declared independence, the war was far from over. In western South Carolina, the Cherokees decided to fight for the British. They attacked many colonists' homes. South Carolina's militia took off after the Cherokees and killed about 2,000 of them. The remaining Cherokees agreed to turn over their lands in the Up Country to South Carolina.

Edward Rutledge signed the Declaration of Independence as a representative of South Carolina.

The Revolutionary War lasted eight years. More than 130 battles were fought in South Carolina, including several in the waters off the coast. In March 1780, British troops left ships in Charleston Harbor and surrounded the city. This began a **siege,** which lasted 40 days. No one could enter or leave the city. On May 12, the American general in charge of

A scene from the Battle of Cowpens

Charleston gave up the city. The British held Charleston for two and a half years.

Three major battles were fought on South Carolina soil. The British won the Battle of Camden in August 1780. Two months later, at Kings Mountain, the Patriots won. Then, the following January, the Patriots won again at the Battle of Cowpens.

But the British continued to hold Charleston until December 13, 1782. It took years for the city to recover. In 1785, the General Assembly voted to build a new capital in the center of the state. They named the new place Columbia, a name that stands for liberty.

THE ONLY WAY FOR AMERICANS TO FIGHT THE BRITISH IN CHARLESTON WAS for small ragtag bands to make surprise raids into the city. Two South Carolina Patriots became heroes making these raids.

A plantation owner named Francis Marion became known as the Swamp Fox. The British soldiers who controlled Charleston were puzzled by the way he and his men could disappear into the swamps after a raid.

Thomas Sumter was a colonel in the state militia when the British captured Charleston. The British burned Sumter's home. He established several small bands armed with nothing but a few bullets and their anger. Sumter became known as the Gamecock, a rooster that is trained to fight. Fort Sumter, where the Civil War would start 80 years later, was named for Thomas Sumter.

Chapter FIVE

A New State, a New Nation

The Articles of Confederation prescribed America's form of government from 1777 to 1787.

AMERICANS HAD DECLARED THEMSELVES INDEpendent of Britain. Now they had to form a government, even with the war going on.

The Continental Congress decided to make America a collection of strong states held together by a central government with little power. The plan was called the Articles of Confederation. The document was approved in November 1777 and was sent to the states to be approved.

The Articles of Confederation said more about what the central government could not do than what it could do.

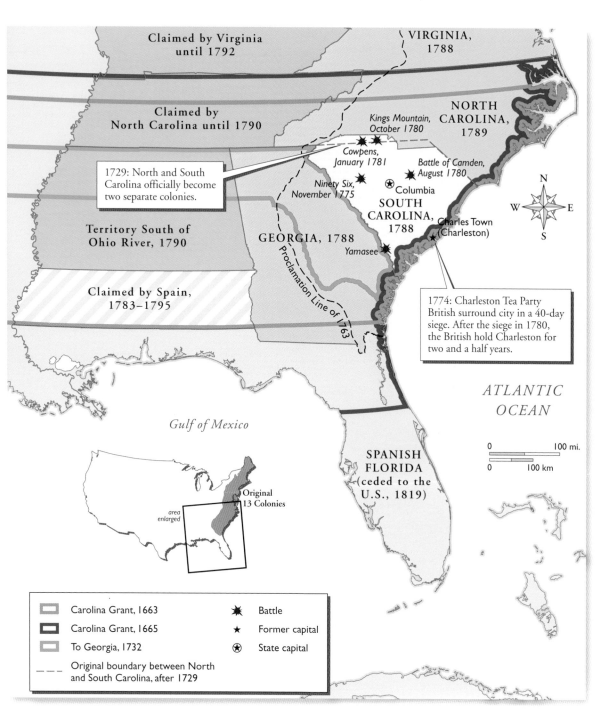

Claimed by Virginia
until 1792

VIRGINIA,
1788

Claimed by
North Carolina until 1790

NORTH
CAROLINA,
1789

Kings Mountain,
October 1780

1729: North and South
Carolina officially become
two separate colonies.

Cowpens,
January 1781

Battle of Camden,
August 1780

Ninety Six,
November 1775

Columbia

Territory South of
Ohio River, 1790

SOUTH
CAROLINA,
1788

N

W   E

S

Charles Town
(Charleston)

GEORGIA, 1788

Claimed by Spain,
1783–1795

Yamasee

1774: Charleston Tea Party
British surround city in a 40-day
siege. After the siege in 1780,
the British hold Charleston for
two and a half years.

Proclamation Line of 1763

ATLANTIC
OCEAN

Gulf of Mexico

SPANISH
FLORIDA
(ceded to the
U.S., 1819)

Original
13 Colonies

area
enlarged

0   100 mi.

0   100 km

Carolina Grant, 1663   ✹   Battle

Carolina Grant, 1665   ★   Former capital

To Georgia, 1732   ✪   State capital

- - -   Original boundary between North
and South Carolina, after 1729

And it couldn't do very much. It did not even
have the power to pass taxes. This meant that
there was no money to pay for anything.

*South Carolina Colony
before statehood*

33

Christopher Gadsden attended the Constitutional Convention as a delegate from South Carolina.

When the Continental army finally defeated the British, many soldiers did not get paid.

Finally, in 1787, the states admitted that the government was not working. They needed a stronger central government with the power to tax. South Carolina sent four delegates, or representatives, to another meet- ing in Philadelphia. The delegates at this meeting would come up with a new plan for a government.

The plan they drew up is now known as the U.S. Constitution. However, the delegates knew that the plan had problems. For example, it said nothing about the rights of individuals. So they came up with the Bill of Rights, which became the first 10 **amendments** to the Constitution, to fix this problem. The Bill of Rights ensures individual rights, such as freedom of speech and freedom of religion.

On September 17, 1787, the delegates signed the new U.S. Constitution. The following May, South Carolina's leaders met in Charleston to approve it. The Up Country farmers tended to be very independent. They wanted a government that would stay out of their business, so they did not like the new constitution. But more people lived in the Low Country, and they voted in favor.

On May 23, 1788, South Carolina became the eighth state to approve the U.S. Constitution. It went into effect in 1789. The new United States of America was born.

Charles Pinckney was one of the delegates from South Carolina at the Constitutional Convention in 1787.

1400s About 29 separate Native American groups live in what is now South Carolina.

1521 Spaniard Francisco Gordillo explores the Carolina coast.

1526 Spaniard Lucas Vásquez de Ayllón builds the first European settlement in South Carolina. It lasts three years.

1562 Frenchman Jean Ribault forms a short-lived colony near Port Royal Sound.

1587 The Spanish withdraw from Carolina.

1663 King Charles II of England gives Carolina to eight men known as the Lords Proprietors.

1670 Carolina's first British settlers establish a settlement on the Ashley River at Albemarle Point. It is soon moved to where Charleston is now.

1671 The first boatload of enslaved Africans arrives in South Carolina.

1712 Carolina is divided into North and South Carolina, each with its own governor.

1715 War breaks out between the Yamasee people and European settlers, resulting in many deaths on both sides.

1738 Eliza Lucas begins growing indigo.

1774 The Charleston Tea Party takes place when rebels dump tea into the harbor to protest taxes.

1780 The British gain control of Charleston after a 40-day siege.

1781 Patriots win the Battle of Cowpens.

1788 South Carolina becomes the eighth state to approve the U.S. Constitution.

1790 The state capital is moved from Charleston to Columbia.

Glossary TERMS

amendments (uh-MEND-muhntst)
Amendments are changes to a constitution.
The Bill of Rights became the first 10
amendments to the U.S. Constitution.

assembly (uh-SEM-blee)
An assembly is a part of government that
makes laws. Early settlers in Carolina
created an assembly in Charleston.

charter (CHAR-tuhr)
A charter is a document giving settlers
permission to form a colony. The Carolina
colony's first charter said laws needed to
be confirmed by white male landowners.

constitution (kon-stuh-TOO-shun)
A constitution is a document describing
a government. At the beginning of the
Revolutionary War, South Carolinians
wrote a state constitution.

**Continental Congress (kon-tuh-NIHN-
tuhl KON-griss)**
The Continental Congress was a meeting
of colonists that served as the American
government around the time of the
Revolution. Representatives at the meeting
wrote a letter protesting their lack of rights.

malaria (muh-LAIR-ee-uh)
Malaria is a serious disease that is spread
by mosquitoes. Several of the early settlers
in the Carolina colony died of malaria.

Parliament (PAR-luh-muhnt)
Parliament is the lawmaking part of the
British government. Residents of the
Carolina colony had to appeal to
Parliament to regain their religious
freedom after 1703.

proprietors (pruh-PRY-uh-torz)
Proprietors were people given ownership
of a colony. In 1663, King Charles II
gave control of the Carolina colony to
the eight Lords Proprietors.

siege (SEEJ)
A siege is when the military refuses to
let any people or supplies in or out of a
city. In March 1780, British troops began
a 40-day siege of Charleston.

37

South Carolina Colony's FOUNDING FATHERS

Pierce Butler (1744–1822)
Continental Congress delegate, 1787–88; Constitutional Convention delegate, 1787; U.S. Constitution signer; U.S. senator, 1789–96, 1803–04

William Henry Drayton (1742–1779)
Continental Congress delegate, 1778–79; Articles of Confederation signer

Thomas Heyward Jr. (1746–1809)
Continental Congress delegate, 1776–78; Declaration of Independence signer; Articles of Confederation signer; justice of criminal court, 1778–80, 1781–89

Richard Hutson (1748–1795)
State house of representatives member, 1776–1779, 1781, 1782, 1785, 1788; Continental Congress delegate, 1778–79; Articles of Confederation delegate; South Carolina lieutenant governor, 1782–83

Henry Laurens (1724–1792)
Continental Congress delegate, 1777–79; Continental Congress president, 1777–78; Articles of Confederation signer

John Matthews (1744–1802)
Continental Congress, 1778–81; Articles of Confederation signer; South Carolina governor, 1782–83

Charles Pinckney (1757–1824)
Constitutional Convention delegate, 1777–78, 1784–87; U.S. Constitution signer; South Carolina state legislature member, 1779–80, 1786–89, 1792–96; South Carolina governor, 1789–92, 1796–98, 1806–08; U.S. senator 1798–1801; U.S. House of Representatives member, 1818–21

Charles Cotesworth Pinckney (1746–1825)
South Carolina state senate member, 1779–1804; Constitutional Convention delegate, 1787; U.S. Constitution signer; U.S. House of Representatives member, 1819–21

Edward Rutledge (1749–1800)
Continental Congress delegate, 1774–77; Declaration of Independence signer; South Carolina legislature member, 1782–96; South Carolina governor, 1798–1800

John Rutledge (1739–1800)
Continental Congress delegate, 1774–76, 1782–83; South Carolina president, 1776–78; South Carolina governor, 1779–82; Constitutional Convention delegate, 1787; U.S. Constitution signer; U.S. supreme court associate justice, 1789–91; South Carolina state supreme court justice, 1790; U.S. supreme court chief justice, 1795

For Further INFORMATION

Web Sites

Visit our homepage for lots of links about the South Carolina colony:
http://www.childsworld.com/links.html

Note to Parents, Teachers, and Librarians:
We routinely verify our Web links to make sure they're safe,
active sites—so encourage your readers to check them out!

Books

Currie, Stephen. *Life of a Slave on a Southern Plantation.* San Diego: Lucent Books, 2000.

Hakim, Joy. *From Colonies to Country.* New York: Oxford University Press, 2003.

Kent, Deborah. *How We Lived . . . in the Southern Colonies.* Tarrytown, N.Y.: Benchmark Books, 2000.

Stein, R. Conrad. *South Carolina.* Danbury, Conn.: Children's Press, 1999.

Places to Visit or Contact

Middleton Place
To learn about life on an 18th-century plantation
4300 Ashley River Road
Charleston, SC 29414
843/556-6020

South Carolina State Museum
To see Native American tools, colonial weapons, and lots of other items from South Carolina's history
301 Gervais Street
Columbia, SC 29201
803/898-4921

Index

About the Author

JEAN F. BLASHFIELD IS THE AUTHOR OF MORE THAN 100 BOOKS, most of them for young people. She has traveled widely and has lived in Chicago, London, and Washington, D.C. She now lives in Wisconsin—at least that's where her house is. Her mind and her computer take her all over the world (and sometimes beyond).